among the enemies

Michael Samra

AN INLANDIA INSTITUTE PUBLICATION

RIVERSIDE, CALIFORNIA

Permissions
Inlandia Institute
4178 Chestnut Street
Riverside CA 92501

Book layout & design: Mark Givens

Printed and bound in the United States
Distributed by Ingram

Library of Congress Cataloging-in-Publication Data

Names: Samra, Michael, author.
Title: Among the enemies / by Michael Samra.
Description: First edition. | Riverside, California : Inlandia Books, [2022] | Summary: "In among the enemies, National Winner of the 2020 Hillary Gravendyk Prize selected by contest judge Maureen Alsop, readers are travelled to the places where the living talk to their wound(s) and take it to the 'show.' The river bides refuge, the omnipresent bells--an origin of distraction, rung for and by the unknown--are a reminder. 'The bells are ringing and I have to pretend I can't hear if I want to get any work done.' And what does the distraction dictate against the toll? Reality, filled with tension for an unsuspecting reader, unfolds discomfort, the dilemma of a mind deteriorating which preserves consciousness into a disturbing dimension"-- Provided by publisher.
Identifiers: LCCN 2021060737 | ISBN 9781955969086 (paperback)
Subjects: LCGFT: Poetry.
Classification: LCC PS3619.A465 A82 2022 | DDC 811/.6--dc23/eng/2021121
LC record available at https://lccn.loc.gov/2021060737

Published by Inlandia Institute
Riverside, California
www.InlandiaInstitute.org
First Edition

among the enemies

Michael Samra

Contents

1

exposure

Everything I've seen you've seen
        our enemies have seen
must have seen some bad things if they
        are our enemies this badly.
They are wrapped around the glare from
        the streetlight I stand under
        convalescing.
I, with seeing, who sees
a knife. Coming this way from the distance.
Someone says relax

A train pulls in howling. Adjacent
        blades of grass tilt
the night murk stuck to one's skin
My favorite shirt a red mess in a
        dumpster somewhere.
Faces hang hard in the dark

Down the street that way is a cloud
        of roaches
so I guess I'll go to this show.
Someone I know has an injury
        how's it doing
Does it want to see the band play

Slept in a shadow a moment
watching the sun go down on
        the big river.
The train all scabrous groaning
        back and forth.
Now that the bells are ringing
I think I can die but that's false.
People walking along a wall
        Still it never ends
I'll still roll things down the hill
towards our enemies and towards town.
For a second someone passed
        in front of the sun

Now that the bells are ringing
the river is also ringing. I don't.
I bet our enemies spend a lot of time
        watching the water.
Now that the bells are ringing I probably
am allowed to die.
so I watch the same boats
        the same river. Helicopters.

This beach infested with our
        enemies. One considers hiding
in sand but sand hides in you.
The sun tumbling in waves
finally rises and something dead is
        stuck to it

It's cold at night when it turns cold
the air comes off the water I
        extend my arm towards the cold

I'm awake in the sand in the face of
        the sand. No one
can unplug it not the waves either. A cloud
        of medical professionals drop on us
where we are having dreams that
        we are on the beach being dragged
        through the sand like strangers

At times like these it's discovered
one wasn't dreaming, had
in fact collapsed on the beach

under the exhaustion of this city
        and its constant danger
of our enemies. In such an instance the
sun sinks into skin and poisons
        it with red swelling.
The hospital fills with
        black coughs and agonies
        of crisp skin
Peeling sheets of fluorescent light
but also, brief escape from our enemies

Nature of injuries
and illnesses inflicted by our enemies
        such that
one never knows secretly if one did it
        oneself. This and
a thousand tricks like this, did I
only for example
        fall asleep in the sun
Was it the sun or our enemies

Our bodies dissolving
        in hospital beds our
enemies at the window. I haven't seen
the medical professionals in days
        I'm drenched

in darkness. A hospital deserted
        by budget cuts
or our enemies. Still it never ends
        so I guess I'll go to this show
so I'll watch the same boats in the dark
hallways I probably watched
on the river. So the train drools

witnessing through windows
what must be how that injury feels
        about its person
incapacitated, dissolving in red mist

boats pass glowing. Days are
        closer together than people think.
In the halls of the shuttered hospital
shadows lurk behind fake trees.
The hallways go hungry.
Out the window the earth churns.
As if the voices out there and in here
        could be assuaged into silence
if only I or someone bled on them.
I licked my lips
I slept on my side that day and let
        the roaches float over my heart

The passageways smell like stale air
but the river's still out there.
Anything could turn out to be
        a statue. I begin

feeling for a door and find it and
        I guess arrive too early
for the show and have to leave.
That knife is flying right towards us

There is no moon and this fog is
dense. I, also
surprised to find beneath
        my convalescence
not in a rush to go anywhere but
        ejected from the empty hospital
like anyone, almost
like our enemies would be
        if they were allowed inside.
Out in the exposed world things
        make noises
The sun is twitching

The city after all is shadows and
        their inverse. Silvery noons
one walks past construction sites
onto bright green grass.
But I live with this injured person
        and their injury and I relate
mold on the ceiling and exposed nails
        as if anyone is better than
the city itself, which is outside
and the dangers in it:
        our enemies, even
that sun-hit grass has roaches.
So then the night rolls across them
and scattered conversations

More blood on the floor than ever.
It's dark, someone untie me.
I begin to be my sections. Every
        moment of blood I have snaps
        and sparkles. Behind which I
think about having someone by the
        river to which to say hello. Still

it never ends, people walking
        along a wall with our enemies
Later I find the wall strangled.
My intestines rise to my eyes and sparkle

Still it never ends.
What an awful environment I must have
selected if I am really here

In the distance:
whispering, and additionally
        a knife with a single handle.
How is your injury does it want to see
        the band play
does it know where the band is playing or
        do we have to ask someone

And the roaches and I am awake in
        the sand in the face of the sand
        with questions.
We are whispering about the
        bells that are ringing
        It's perfect.
Trains go by but I'm
        inside them sometimes or everyone
        and roaches
and I stand in the sand stretching
        our unimportances.
We are whispering that the bells are
        perfect

Move blood across the floor forever.
By the river it says hello
Days like this think about our enemies
          and say relax
while in the distance I'm sicking up.
They say it like strangers

A dirty night, deodorant
          settles like mist
onto brick walls and sidewalks
not liking the way it sticks to me.
Our enemies are always the way
          they are but not always

Oncoming traffic, it never ends
the mouths of the roaches loudly dry
Our enemies hang like icicles from ledges
leaving the city less populous.
Someone leaning out a window
        gets demolished.

On the train there is someone crying
        It's very hard
to go on. The river impaled by boats
        is waiting for our eyes to look at it.
But I've taken on this task of observing
as I have been and studying our enemies

This report will be useful

In the museum hiding from
snow and from our enemies
there are etchings on display.
At the grocery store the produce
is always wrinkled and there's an etching
        of that which everyone can relate to.
My mother called in the morning
but didn't mention the etching of
        the river was so good.
There was a pigeon also on the tiled floor
which had gotten inside
        but which was not an etching

Out of my distance exorcises a
        restaurant our enemies patronized.
I am out in the world
in search of protection
at the banks of the river shaking
        trees throwing bread
        at pigeons. It's starting to rain
I can't remember how rain starts.
But a straight line
that is the river swells

One spends a lot of time on trains
over a bridge over the river
        along featureless streets
sometimes in tunnels underground.
Their wheels pant against the tracks
        and on occasion screech.
Our enemies are never on the trains, on
the trains sometimes you
can't even see the mountains and
        the city like it doesn't end
even at the forest which it does end at

but which is actually within the city. The
        north part

The story of the humans is
a battle against everything getting
disgusting which we
        are losing.
To think about that sometimes
makes our enemies seem less
        important but they are not.
Our enemies hang like icicles
        over us and fall

One night I'm pulled aside by a knife.
        It wants to talk to me
                It thinks I live
                by the river

I already know more about my sections
        than anyone but the knife
One night I drive the knife into my head
and let the knife describe
        my head

Later the hardness of the train seat
annoys one's bones much like
        the rolling of the black river
annoys the lines of light that try
        to lie down on it

The story of the humans is
disgusting which we
are losing. I also
one night trailed the knife along
        a sidewalk. That night
I slept on my side
and let the roaches fight
        over my heart.
At the edge of the woods
rodents awake and
        rustling

As a direct result
(everyone beginning
        to resemble objects)
of people serving no apparent purpose
except to be in the way
I can't anymore differentiate
        between people and objects.
So into the woods I
        collapse. Little
birds in branches
        like laughter

Our enemies are always
        the way they are but
are not always the way they are
        on purpose.
There is something about the woods
and the traps I set up there
        that is bad for our enemies
to walk into without knowing
        about them.
but there is something
about the woods that I also want
        splinters

These days I'm easy prey
        for our enemies.
By the time I notice they
        aren't objects they're upon me
They blend in with the wallpaper
        and spread out
like they don't care how we make
the guns that are useless
against them. I hope
they aren't in the wallpaper now
because I'm asking if you know
        when does the show start.
Having come across the restaurant
where our enemies one time
        ate, of course
        deserted now

Objects everyone is becoming
        to me and being in the way
        what they do.
At the abandoned restaurant where
        we wait, eyes out for our enemies
air comes in the cracked glass
        window cold and turning gray

Everything out the window under
        thick dew. After breakfast I
am sharpening the special knife.
        It is not useless.
There it is in the distance
just over the horizon heading
        right towards us.
When should we leave for the show

2

experiments

The city its streets today
somehow engorged.
Our enemies did not go away
        despite being defeated so now
we must figure out what to do with them.
The train disposes of evidence
        circling. Still it never ends
The month of the roaches' lagging taste
        and getting off the train who here
        isn't objects that I hate

The bells are ringing better than ever so
        probably I can die except for
our enemies still are alive and obscuring
        noises with their own noises
even though kept in line
        by my knife's constant
        destruction of them.

So, what is to be done
        gets on the mind.
First to organize them into separate
        containers for interrogating.
Through windows watching them
        in containers we will
        figure out how they work

First investigating with dogs
the neon sign outside always changing
        colors
insinuating something will happen.
Still it never ends.
So what is it that gets on the mind
So wow. I vent on some trees
using the special knife to destroy them.
When they were free
our enemies didn't solve our problems
        our problems being
        that our enemies were free so
now they are locked up.
For observation

It's cold and when it turns cold
        the air rolls in off the water
impressed by all the neon signs
        and the objects.
Our enemies multiplying
        despite that they are locked up
        and kept also separate
Their cages multiplying also. This mystery
is very hard to look at
I look at a mountain in my distances to
        discuss.
I look at it to excess. The bells
are ringing and I have to pretend
I can't hear if I want to get any work
        done. Our enemies
sometimes more trouble locked up
than when they weren't

So what is it, that grass by the road.
What will it do to our enemies if we feed
them
        it. These questions are the kind
that make someone good at what I do
and that I ask. For the answers
        we go to our enemies
        and do it at them.
Meantime the people I work with

do they even want to go to the show
        I can't tell so instead
        ask our enemies
by way of massive experiments on them.
So wow they have interesting answers for me

but none as coherent as their eyes dropping
        into their intestines

So, they have intestines. Answers that.
        But what about this
the way they eat that grass and the weeds.
Forehead against the window
I slept inside the observatory that
        day and let the fluorescent lights
        puddle on the floor.
Too early to snow.
I remembered something I don't remember
        right now
Leaning out the window

So for now I still have intestines.
interesting sensation.
While in the park feeding pigeons
         their own blood
Today this idea occurs that we
shall have our enemies vote
         which of them shall decide
which of them don't get dropped
off the roof. Based on the results
         of that experiment we will then
drop all of them off the roof.
         to observe their reaction.
An effort to better understand them

One night I take the knife for a walk.
I notice that shadows are licking it, how
         strange are shadows

One of our enemies I'm in charge of
        giving a whole extra set of bones
into its body.
I'm just on a train
minding my own business
        and this sound comes out of my face
that matches the contortion of my face.
Pretty heinous.
One night all of these objects surround
        me at a bar and want to celebrate
the success of an experiment

but I'm tired, tomorrow
        must early start
watching chemicals affect our enemies.
All that's lacking is more shadows

It's astonishing sometimes that anyone
        could be as evil as
        our enemies and still
be affected by these experiments.
Of course they react mostly
        differently than we would
but they do share a surprising amount
        of reactions, such as
permanent bodily strangeness and
        not liking when we
        throw things at them.
At first I liked my position
but what if there is no logic to it.
That's something nobody would say
        out loud; here it is in my report

Some days I notice my face is
shrieking again on a train before I
        remember there's people around
and just because they are objects
doesn't mean that they are

To describe the observatory it
        is a large dome the first floor
filled with our enemies in separate
        containers the second floor
and up is rooms with glass
        floors, the reason I'm always
lying on the floor because observing.

One night all these objects
        harangue me through
the glass thinking
I remember something they don't

Today's task is removing
        a subject's entire body
and switching it with another.
This takes hours and
many hands so it's abandoned
        halfway
and replaced with the idea of
removing their emotions, easier
but less satisfying. The subjects
tend to ooze for months after.
We wanted to turn them different
        colors

One night harassed by objects after
a day at work and a night
at the bar. A new experiment
involves sewing certain numbers of our
          enemies together
to see if combining them assists them
          in no longer being so foul.
I can't remember today how
          to walk normal
I am loud on trains so much the
          bells sound faint.
One night I hear music getting off
          the train. Is it the show has
          it started already

I'm in charge in addition to my other
        duties of smashing indefinitely
        the head of one of our enemies.
The hypothesis is that it will have no effect
A hypothesis I am beginning to doubt.
I'm so exhausted I divert
        this particular task
onto its particular enemy, leaving it there
        on the beach to smash its own head
indefinitely. That was by now an
        uncertain amount of time ago

If not objects it is
the medical professionals
        returning finally
to check on me only my condition
        hasn't changed. In all
the goings-on what if
        we've already missed the show

One set of our enemies was one day required
to drink air and breathe dirt they
          reacted to this immensely.
A turning point in our research, something
I'd like to take credit for
but was instead the idea of the boy
          I am in love with and dream
of dissecting. A boy that no one likes.
In response I destroy all my subjects
          with incendiary bombs and
          demand some more

So what is it about the woods that keeps
          distracting me by wanting
to invent ways to drench them in darkness.
The bells are ringing so great today

I've got a great new experiment
where I study our enemies individually
and conceive of very thoughtful gifts
        crafted specially to please them
then give them each their gift and after
        they unwrap the gift
and are pleased I shoot them

and then extract the brains
        to see how they did it.
Then I dismantle those ones' bodies. The sun
sets nicely these days so it's good
one doesn't have to hide under tables

Putting warts all over them one afternoon
        I get thoughtful.
When I was a child of course someone
        would regularly knock me down
and pull all the veins out
        of my arm and dangle them
in front of me and make me look at them.
A few years later one time also
but then afterwards I was
        completely recovered.
So I do have a lot of experience

Flicking the lights off and on
        to see if our enemies
        would still be there.
One idea, a small
        apartment was built
in the abdomen of one of our enemies
and one of us moved in there for a month.
Although only their head fit
The subject displayed
        gnashings of teeth
and leaking but few conclusive results

A bird murmurs at sundown.
Apartment buildings take on
        a bluishness
The light goes on over a door.
Cars look silky
        and double-parked, soothing
after an evening thick with experiments.
Informed our enemies today
        about the bacteria
growing naturally in their containers.
        If you see anything on the walls
        that's pink
or orange it is deadly

So what is it that once done
          gets on the mind.
The lights at night outside
          wavering afraid
of the places their bodies don't
touch. It reminded me as I
          walked home
late and aching of an experiment
where the insides of some enemies
          were made to glow in the dark
and then they were left in the dark.
The idea was to turn our enemies
          into light sources to see
if they could in this way be put
to some use. They did not glow
          however or survive

One night forgot
my family was celebrating
something I forgot. Cheerful voices
asking about my work. It
is hard to explain and not glamorous
although interesting
          and absolutely necessary.
I pour a drink into a cup
then drink it. That afternoon on break
I'd gone to the park. Three ducks
by the little river on the grass
in and out of tree-shadows and sun.
I took a picture of them.
The picture came out awful

The new policy is to solve
our personal problems first on our enemies.
Really only desiring answers
The good idea to feed them only vinegar
        made me have to lie down
by the river near the sun. I like the way
the sun makes me feel beige
and the world red and heaving
        when I'm lying
in that spot just then. It's good
now that our enemies aren't looming
        loose in the world

We turn their blood into different
things anything so long
        as it is not blood.
Most days
it doesn't occur to me to observe
their faces since they barely
are faces. Today though
by accident. Still
        it never ends
not their faces wriggling
or the blood changes. I must have
Did not have coffee.
I started to scratch my head with
        the knife
then remembered it was the knife

Mostly threatening to swallow
        me up the days keep
shrinking. A party is the same as
being alone in a room full of objects
        with party hats on them.
People have to hold their heads in
        sunlight to keep
        from becoming no good.
A plane flies low over the city
into one of the mountains

I am at this point one of those
        on my stomach, on the floor
observing through the glass.
None of the day's experiments
        are pleasing so
we carve holes in a frozen lake
and jam them in there upside down to see
how their skulls react.
The ice smells like a hospital hallway
I should know

It was a busy day so
we lured them with fake prostitutes and
        when they fell for it
hit them with crazy hallucinogens.
Through tubes into their cages we
inserted wind to escort them around
in vivid somersaults. Then had them
        lie in cold sludge
        and not talk to each other
then blindfolded them
and had them fight, arranged them
in trees and contemplated them
Then introduced starving dogs
        into the branches. Later
We put them back in the cages
        where the ceilings spat fire

So what is it that dances
now that the bells are ringing
        when it wants
to be dead. I also turn and the exhaustion
that carries people off in
        the middle of things.

We put our enemies into tunnels of black ooze
        and watch them socialize

Then set their stomachs on fire

so many square miles of skin.
After all the pigeons strut
featuring their own blood

3

expurgation

Bits of sunlight stream
        through the window
as if they are singing.
the floor moves closer then
        farther away moves
miles of blood across itself.
I'm almost certain we missed
        the show and anyway
probably the injury can't make it.
So instead I'll go to the river
look at the sky and think to myself
the levee is so great to look at
        in this light

That was the night I was
        digging and digging
        in the sand all day.
I volunteered. I liked to watch
the moon go up while standing
        with a shovel on the beach.
It's one of those memories you later
        remember when you can't
remember what you're remembering.
Still it never ends
the bells are ringing so hard
In a dark house it's dark somewhere
        in the woods
I had to be tied up. I tie myself up

On the levee if that's what you call it
like something needing a brain
        that watches the sunset because
it has to. I don't want people thinking
I was either last to notice
        or first I don't like either
and between those two seems too vast
        and hungry

" Today instructed our enemies
to swallow the insides of their heads "
reads my journal " they are sometimes
        more locked up than
        they weren't "
I get chills. I hear the train

I volunteered. I liked to watch
the moon stand up while
burying things on the beach.
        The sand
filling up with their dead selves

I can't get near the train
Some asshole tells me not to feed
        the pigeons
It's hard to locate exactly when
        our enemies were finally gone

It was some time, I remember, between
        experiments. And they were

Now I've never been so far behind
          the river
I follow on gray noons the glass
that fell off the restaurant windows
The woods are silent

Even my traps shout echoes at
          each other and sob.
Walking those sapped paths
Dawns come too soon and are vacant
My favorite shirt washes up
It's got a lot of holes in it

Little bits of trees here and there
as I walk through the woods
crumbling into embers
and by the river three ducks float
        inexplicably dead.
Everyone has to make their
        own decisions.
There is something about the ducks
something about the trees
        falling over, eaten through
by little flames

I spit on the special knife and put it
          on a sailboat.
One of our enemies would have
          right now
been required to cry on a train
          or count ice cubes fast
on a hot day. Would have been
required right now. The passages
reek of meat I hear music the show
does the injury want to see the band
          play

It gets lonely
ships every dawn launch
        skittering from the harbor

people going elsewhere
        differently than we would
leaving behind the sounds
and all of the things we look at
        things with.
Now it's even possible
to walk down your street and no one
        knows what you're
        talking about

so I take the streets
at odd hours to see what shapes
        objects have

I take the streets at odd hours to
        see what shapes I have.
Now it's oddly possible
to walk down to the neon sign
and see the mountains
even from there, discolored
and see no one. I begin
        the long walk:
it's easily likely
our enemies are only hiding
        behind all molecules
        isn't it

and only appear to be
        exterminated.
But wouldn't they have
        shown themselves
        by now

How strange to
watch your shadow whipped
        by the wind
I am almost certain the show
is happening somewhere around here
        and also that things move
in ways only I care about seeing

and there is the knife, in the distance
        in a sailboat

I pass the hospital, collapsed
        the grocery store
and the observatory, collapsed.
So far I still have intestines

In the middle of the collapsed hospital
        I give myself a trophy
it is a piece of the wallpaper
which I toyed with by the sky
        moving fast its clouds
try to eat. And choke

a cricket chirps outside the hospital
        and it is hard not to think
that the cricket has taken over
in front of me and made me look at it.
But I've taken on this task of observing

when I buried our enemies on the beach
        by the river and said hello.
Now I want to know who's ringing
        the bells

At the venue finally
It's almost certain the show is over
          or somehow hasn't started
or is so boring that it is nothing
and no one showed up not even the band.
The venue is empty
On the sticky black floor flyers flip idly
like they're playing a game
          and one's shoes are hard to pry off it.
An injury alone on the linoleum like trash
          but no sign of its person

The nothingness of the show operates a
        twisting sensation on the brain
until lack of oxygen
and the slow vortex of it convinces one
the room is packed with people
        the smell of sweat and noise
        flashing lights like
white roses pop on the ceiling.
But there's nothing, the venue as
        empty as if out of business.
Only stepping outside
one's head clears, maybe

Consider in the venue bodies strung up
          on the ceiling, lights
glance through stomach linings.
Still it never ends
in those moments where the sweat lives
you see stomachs on hooks
          where the ceiling glows dull
through the linings, sometimes strobed
          which the dancers like.
They drip a bit which the band can drink.
That musk of many bodies in there
so that one's shirt
          can stick to one's back

The crowd fluctuates
like grass on the side of the highway.
They have intestines
          They're lining up
at the bar for syrupy drinks.
From the ceiling fan dangle veins
with a pink film on them, someone
daring someone else to lick it.
The lights go on and off

In turns returning to and rejecting
        the venue
into and out of thinking
        I should check again
Maybe the show is starting or
is it long over
I reenter then exit but even outside the
sticky linoleum and peeling
walls cling to the inside
of one's head and the inside of the head
is still inside the venue. Is
        replaced by the venue.
I see the blurry faces faceless.
Or are all those objects in there
actually people. I have to go sit
        by the river

Helicopters, the sun tumbles
        flickering in the waves.
I'm awake in the sand and the face
        agape, shiny
like medical professionals with
hushed discussions by a window.
The sun twitches across the sand
like strangers distracted
by the odd whistling of
        things that don't move

at night
Standing at the sink but not sure why
        A new way of looking
at bugs instead of sleeping.

and when I see a roach I pour water on it
and it goes down the drain but always
there's another and often
        that one I don't catch
but then I find another
        somewhere else, already dead

ACKNOWLEDGMENTS

Our enemies and I would like to extend gratitude to many persons, including: Cati Porter and everyone at Inlandia Institute, as well as Maureen Alsop, for making it all possible ; the memory and work of Hillary Gravendyk, with whom it's an honor to be associated, and Megan Gravendyk-Estrella ; Ben Lerner, and Anselm Berrigan, for expertise and sympathy regarding pigeon encounters as well as other matters ; Brendan Lorber for the protection offered on occasion at his castle across from the necropolis, during the early tumultuous years ; Bridget Tunnel John Kropa Lancelot Runge and Mariette Lamson for their undying loyalty ; Sarah VanDermeer, painter of this book's cover and creator of many other visuals and tangibles, connoisseur of spiderwebs ; and first of all, thanks to everyone, but zero and especially no thanks specifically to Anahit Gulian, my loathsome and nefarious nemesis who must be stopped at any cost. Endless gratitude to George and Marge Samra, and to the Smiths, more than anyone, for always knowing where I live ; to Heather for Heather and for everything ; to Heather still and also to Jon Patten and to Sarah Vandermeer again for assistance in evading a bloody death immediately prior to the writing of this book. And most of all to Patrick Song, for his essential, unflagging, and possibly unsettling dedication to the enemies from the start.

ABOUT THE AUTHOR

Michael Samra is a poet, writer, and painter. His work has appeared in *Bennington Review*, *Coastal Shelf*, and a number of other publications; a finalist for the Anhinga-Robert Dana Prize, he's received the Himan Brown Award and the 2020 Hillary Gravendyk Prize. Having previously resided in New York, Philadelphia, and elsewhere, he lives at present in New Orleans on a segment of railroad tracks disturbed on occasion by the train, which appears to be some kind of demigod.

ABOUT THE HILLARY GRAVENDYK PRIZE

The Hillary Gravendyk Prize is an open poetry book competition published by Inlandia Institute for all writers regardless of the number of previously published poetry collections.

HILLARY GRAVENDYK (1979-2014) was a beloved poet living and teaching in Southern California's "Inland Empire" region. She wrote the acclaimed poetry book, *HARM* from Omnidawn Publishing (2012) and the posthumoussly published *The Soluble Hour* (Omnidawn, 2017) and *Unlikely Conditions* (1913 Press, 2017, with Cynthia Arrieu-King) as well as the poetry chapbook *The Naturalist* (Anchiote Press, 2008). A native of Washington State, she was an admired Assistant Professor of English at Pomona College in Claremont, CA. Her poetry has appeared widely in journals such as *American Letters & Commentary, The Bellingham Review, The Colorado Review, The Eleventh Muse, Fourteen Hills, MARY, 1913: A Journal of Forms, Octopus Magazine, Tarpaulin Sky* and *Sugar House Review*. She was awarded a 2015 Pushcart Prize for her poem "Your Ghost," which appeared in the Pushcart Prize Anthology. She leaves behind many devoted colleagues, friends, family and beautiful poems. Hillary Gravendyk passed away on May 10, 2014 after a long illness. This contest has been established in her memory.

ABOUT INLANDIA INSTITUTE

Inlandia Institute is a regional non-profit and literary center. We seek to bring focus to the richness of the literary enterprise that has existed in this region for ages. The mission of the Inlandia Institute is to recognize, support, and expand literary activity in all of its forms in Inland Southern California by publishing books and sponsoring programs that deepen people's awareness, understanding, and appreciation of this unique, complex and creatively vibrant region.

The Institute publishes books, presents free public literary and cultural programming, provides in-school and after school enrichment programs for children and youth, holds free creative writing workshops for teens and adults, and boot camp intensives. In addition, every two years, the Inlandia Institute appoints a distinguished jury panel from outside of the region to name an Inlandia Literary Laureate who serves as an ambassador for the Inlandia Institute, promoting literature, creative literacy, and community. Laureates to date include Susan Straight (2010-2012), Gayle Brandeis (2012-2014), Juan Delgado (2014-2016), Nikia Chaney (2016-2018), and Rachelle Cruz (2018-2020).

To learn more about the Inlandia Institute, please visit our website at www.InlandiaInstitute.org.

OTHER HILLARY GRAVENDYK PRIZE BOOKS

This Side of the Fire by Jonathan Maule
Winner of the 2020 National Hillary Gravendyk Prize

The Silk the Moths Ignore by Bronwen Tate
Winner of the 2019 National Hillary Gravendyk Prize

Remyth: A Postmodern Ritual by Adam D. Martinez
Winner of the 2019 Regional Hillary Gravendyk Prize

All the Emergency-Type Structures by Elizabeth Cantwell
Winner of the 2018 Regional Hillary Gravendyk Prize

Our Bruises Kept Singing Purple by Malcolm Friend
Winner of the 2017 National Hillary Gravendyk Prize

Traces of a Fifth Column by Marco Maisto
Winner of the 2016 National Hillary Gravendyk Prize

God's Will for Monsters by Rachelle Cruz
Winner of the 2016 Regional Hillary Gravendyk Prize
Winner of a 2018 American Book Award

Map of an Onion by Kenji C. Liu
Winner of the 2015 National Hillary Gravendyk Prize

All Things Lose Thousands of Times by Angela Peñaredondo
Winner of the 2015 Regional Hillary Gravendyk Prize